KEY FIGURES OF
THE WARS IN IRAQ AND AFGHANISTAN

★ BIOGRAPHIES OF WAR ★

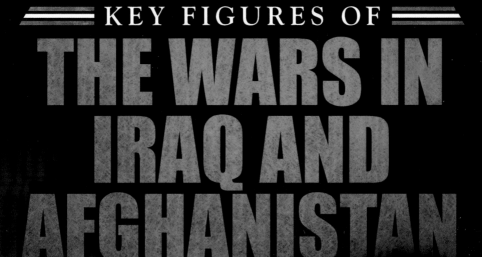
KEY FIGURES OF
THE WARS IN IRAQ AND AFGHANISTAN

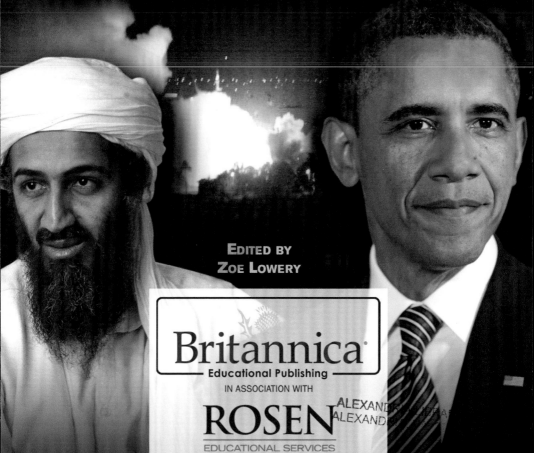

EDITED BY
ZOE LOWERY

Britannica®
Educational Publishing
IN ASSOCIATION WITH

ROSEN
EDUCATIONAL SERVICES

ALEXAND
ALEXAND

Published in 2016 by Britannica Educational Publishing (a trademark of Encyclopædia Britannica, Inc.) in association with The Rosen Publishing Group, Inc.
29 East 21st Street, New York, NY 10010

Distributed exclusively by Rosen Publishing.
To see additional Britannica Educational Publishing titles, go to rosenpublishing.com.

First Edition

Britannica Educational Publishing
J.E. Luebering: Director, Core Reference Group
Anthony L. Green: Editor, Compton's by Britannica

Rosen Publishing
Hope Lourie Killcoyne: Executive Editor
Zoe Lowery: Editor
Nelson Sá: Art Director
Michael Moy: Designer
Cindy Reiman: Photography Manager
Karen Huang: Photo Researcher
Introduction and supplementary material by Barbara Krasner.

Library of Congress Cataloging-in-Publication Data

Key figures of the wars in Iraq and Afghanistan/edited by Zoe Lowery.—First edition.
      pages cm.—(Biographies of war)
Includes bibliographical references and index.
ISBN 978-1-68048-066-5 (library bound)
1. Iraq War, 2003–2011—Juvenile literature. 2. Persian Gulf War, 1991—Juvenile literature. 3. Afghan War, 2001——Juvenile literature. I. Lowery, Zoe.
DS79.763.K49 2016
956.7044'3—dc23
                                                                        2014043152

Manufactured in the United States of America

CONTENTS

INTRODUCTION 6

CHAPTER ONE
WAR IN AFGHANISTAN   10

CHAPTER TWO
WARS IN IRAQ   20

CHAPTER THREE
KEY FIGURES IN THE WAR IN
AFGHANISTAN   39

CHAPTER FOUR
KEY FIGURES IN THE IRAQ WARS   61

CONCLUSION 96
GLOSSARY 98
FOR MORE INFORMATION 100
BIBLIOGRAPHY 103
INDEX 105

U.S. KILLED IN
TROOPS
IRAQ
N.Y.S. KILLED

On Sept. 11, 2001, in the worst attack on the United States since the bombing of Pearl Harbor in 1941, terrorists struck two major symbols of U.S. commercial and military strength. The terrorists hijacked four commercial airplanes, crashing two of them into the twin towers of the World Trade Center complex in New York City and one into the Pentagon near Washington, D.C.; the fourth plane crashed in western Pennsylvania. The crashes resulted in the destruction of the World Trade Center towers and the southwest side of the Pentagon. In all, about 2,750 people were killed in New York, 184 at the Pentagon,

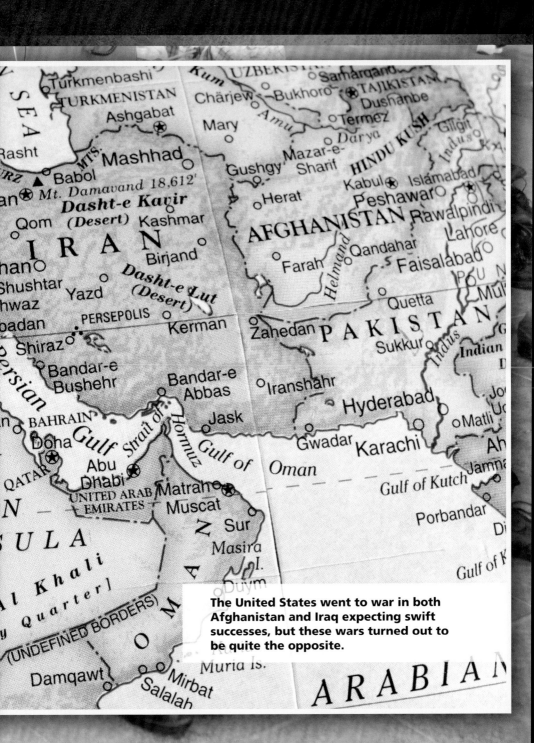

The United States went to war in both Afghanistan and Iraq expecting swift successes, but these wars turned out to be quite the opposite.

and 40 in Pennsylvania. All 19 terrorists died. Osama bin Laden and his al-Qaeda network were believed to be responsible for the attacks—the deadliest terrorist attacks on American soil in U.S. history.

In response to the attacks, U.S. President George W. Bush announced that the country would fight terrorism as the "first war of the 21st century." The United States also called on other governments to join it in an alliance against terrorism by sharing information and supporting each other's efforts to combat terrorist organizations. Soon thereafter the United Nations (UN) Security Council passed a binding resolution requiring its member nations to pursue terrorists and their political and financial supporters. Within a month, the United States declared war on Afghanistan, whose Taliban government it accused of sheltering bin Laden and his terrorist group. By the end of the year the Taliban government had collapsed, but the fighting there continued.

In 2002 President Bush turned the world's attention to Iraq. He accused the government of Iraq of having ties to terrorists and of ignoring a weapons ban that had been imposed on Iraq at the end of the Persian Gulf War in 1991. After the United States brought the matter before the UN in November 2002, Bush declared that Iraq was not cooperating with UN weapons inspectors. While several member countries of the UN Security Council called for further talks between the two sides, the United States and Great Britain threatened to take military action against Iraq. In March 2003 the talks came to an end, and U.S.-led troops invaded Iraq.

Although initially the United States believed it could produce quick victories in both Afghanistan and Iraq, these wars are now among the longest wars in American history. Public opinion, from private citizens to political leaders across the United States, Europe, and elsewhere, has either steadfastly opposed or supported these wars. Although at first there was little opposition to the war against Afghanistan, strong voices have come out against the war in Iraq, creating a global peace movement.

By June 2010 the United States had more troops in Afghanistan than in Iraq, a trend that continued in 2011 (when the U.S. military formally declared the end of its mission in Iraq) and 2012. Events in 2014, however, brought American forces back into Iraq to assist trapped refugees and to prevent the spread of insurgent attacks within and outside of Iraq. The emergence of the Islamic State in Iraq and Syria (ISIS) and its brutal initiatives have stunned leaders and civilians and pose significant threats.

Personalities and egos help shape conflict, and the wars with Afghanistan and Iraq are no exception. The biographies in this volume introduce some of the men and women charged with political and military leadership in these conflicts and describe their rise to power, their specific roles leading up to or during the Afghanistan and Iraq wars, and their support or opposition to them. They also demonstrate the volatile nature of political leadership in Afghanistan and Iraq and the importance of stability.

CHAPTER ONE

WAR IN AFGHANISTAN

The Afghanistan War was an international conflict in Afghanistan beginning in 2001 that was triggered by the September 11 attacks and consisted of three phases. The first phase—toppling the Taliban (the ultra-conservative political and religious faction that ruled Afghanistan and provided sanctuary for al-Qaeda, perpetrators of the September 11 attacks)—was brief, lasting just two months. The second phase (2002–2008) involved a U.S. strategy of defeating the Taliban militarily and rebuilding core institutions of the Afghan state. The third phase began in 2008 and accelerated with U.S. Pres. Barack Obama's 2009 decision to dramatically increase the U.S. troop presence in Afghanistan. The larger force was used to implement a strategy of protecting the population from Taliban attacks and supporting efforts to reintegrate insurgents into Afghan society.

PRELUDE TO THE SEPTEMBER 11 ATTACKS

The joint U.S. and British invasion of Afghanistan in late 2001 was preceded by over two decades of war in Afghanistan. On Dec. 24, 1979, Soviet tanks rumbled across the Amu Darya River and into Afghanistan, ostensibly to restore stability following a coup that brought to power a pair of Marxist-Leninist political groups—the People's (Khalq) Party and the Banner (Parcham) Party. But the Soviet presence touched off a nationwide rebellion by Islamist fighters, who won extensive covert backing from Pakistan, Saudi Arabia, and the United States and who were joined in their fight by foreign volunteers. The guerrilla war against

A convoy of Soviet armoured vehicles crossing a bridge at the Soviet-Afghan border, May 21, 1988, during the withdrawal of the Red Army from Afghanistan.

the Soviet forces led to their departure a decade later. In the void, civil war reigned, with the Islamist fighters—known as the mujahideen—battling first to oust the Soviet-backed government and then turning their guns on each other.

In 1996 the Taliban seized Kabul and instituted a severe interpretation of Islamic law that, for example, forbade female education and prescribed the severing of hands, or even execution, as punishment for petty crimes. That same year, al-Qaeda leader Osama bin Laden was welcomed to Afghanistan (having been expelled from Sudan) and established his organization's headquarters there. With al-Qaeda's help, the Taliban had won control of over 90 percent of Afghan territory by the summer of 2001. On September 9 of that year, al-Qaeda hit men carried out the assassination of famed mujahideen leader Ahmad Shah Massoud, who at the time was leading the Northern Alliance (a loose coalition of mujahideen militias that maintained control of a small section of northern Afghanistan) as it battled the Taliban and who had unsuccessfully sought greater U.S. backing for his efforts.

THE U.S.-BRITISH INVASION

After the September 2001 terrorist attacks on the United States, for which bin Laden was considered the architect, the United States demanded that

THE TALIBAN

After a bloody, decade-long war in Afghanistan, a group intent on establishing a new society based on Islamic law came to power in the mid-1990s. The group was known as the Taliban. Most of the faction's members were former students of religious training institutes set up in the 1980s for Afghan refugees in northern Pakistan.

In addition to enforcing strict Islamic law, known as Sharī ʿah, the Taliban allowed Afghanistan to be a haven for Islamic militants from throughout the world, including an exiled Saudi Arabian, Osama bin Laden, who stood accused of organizing numerous terrorist attacks against U.S. interests. The Taliban's refusal to extradite bin Laden to the United States following the terrorist attacks on the World Trade Center in New York City and the Pentagon outside Washington, D.C., on Sept. 11, 2001, prompted a military confrontation with the United States and allied powers. The U.S.-led forces began aerial attacks on Afghanistan on Oct. 7, 2001, and U.S. special forces were later deployed on the ground. With U.S. backing, the Northern Alliance, an Afghan opposition force that had controlled a small portion of the country in the north, advanced southward on the ground. The Taliban surrendered Kandahār, its political and religious base, on December 7. Taliban control of Afghanistan officially ended on Dec. 9, 2001, after the regime gave up the province of Zabul, its last remaining territory. Bin Laden was eventually killed in a raid by U.S. forces in Pakistan in 2011.

Before the Taliban regime collapsed, some al-Qaeda terrorists took refuge in remote caves such as this one in Afghanistan's Tora Bora mountains.

Afghanistan turn over bin Laden to U.S. authorities, threatening military action for noncompliance. The Taliban refused despite escalating pressure, and in October of that year, the United States, aided by British forces, began an air assault on key military targets in Afghanistan. The two countries provided significant logistical support to Northern Alliance forces in an attempt to force the regime to yield to its demands. Within a month, the Taliban regime began to crumble, and UN-led peacekeeping talks began with members of the Northern Alliance. On December 7 the Taliban surrendered Kandahār, the militia's base of power and the last city under its control. In early December, with the Taliban defeated, Pashtun tribal leader Hamid Karzai was appointed by a UN-led coalition to head an interim government. In 2002 a transitional government was selected to rule the country until national elections could be held and a new constitution drafted.

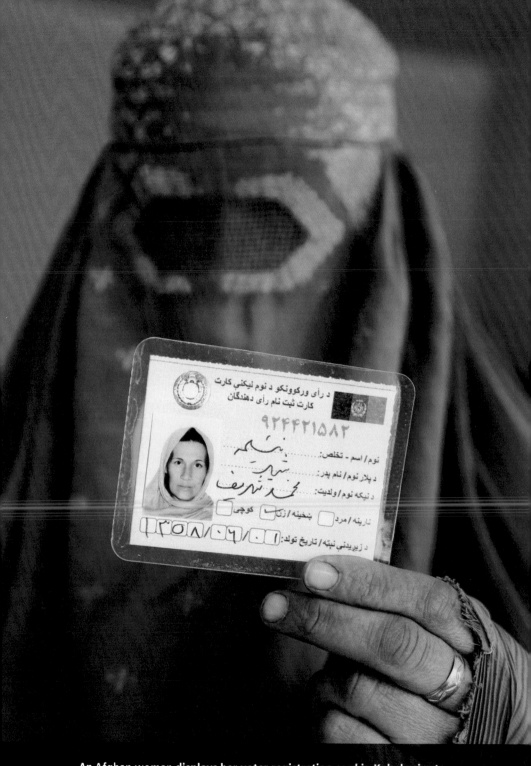

An Afghan woman displays her voter registration card in Kabul prior to

AFGHANISTAN PRESIDENTIAL ELECTIONS

In 2004 a new constitution was written, which called for a directly elected president and a two-chamber legislature. Hamid Karzai, leader of the transitional government, then signed it into law. Democratic elections, in which women were granted the right to vote, were held in October 2004, and Karzai was elected president.

In March 2005 Karzai announced that elections would be held later that year. Although al-Qaeda and Taliban elements had threatened to disrupt the elections, they took place on Sept. 18, 2005. This was the first time in more than 30 years that such elections were held. In December the newly elected National Assembly convened its first session. Ongoing violence throughout 2005 increased steeply at year's end and worsened considerably the following year. Attacks and violent exchanges between the U.S.-led coalition and the Taliban forces became more frequent, and casualties increased. In keeping with campaign statements that the war in Afghanistan would require greater attention and commitment on the part of the United States, newly elected U.S. Pres. Barack Obama announced in February 2009 that some 17,000 additional U.S. troops would be sent to Afghanistan that year.

Karzai's term as president was due to expire in May 2009. However, the approaching presidential election—in which Karzai would be a candidate—

was postponed from May to August of that year. Karzai remained in office until the election.

The presidential election was held on Aug. 20, 2009, and was followed by weeks of political turmoil. With more than 2,000 complaints of fraud and intimidation, suspect polling stations, including those that registered a turnout exceeding 100 percent, were investigated. In mid-October the ECC ruled that the fraudulent activity was widespread enough to invalidate votes from more than 200 polling stations. As a result of the ruling, almost one-third of Karzai's votes were invalidated, and he no longer held the majority he had claimed. A second round of elections was required. Abdullah Abdullah withdrew from the race before elections were held. Karzai was inaugurated as president for a second term.

ACCELERATED AMERICAN INVOLVEMENT

Insurgent attacks increased in 2009. After some debate, Obama announced in December 2009 that the United States would temporarily increase the number of troops in Afghanistan by 30,000. This increase in troop strength would be tied to an accelerated timetable for the training of Afghan security forces and the transfer of security responsibilities from NATO to the Afghan government.

The number of NATO troops in Afghanistan peaked in 2010 at nearly 150,000. The increase in troops delivered mixed results; although NATO troops were able to sweep the Taliban out of areas that it had previously controlled, militants continued to launch devastating surprise attacks against military, government, and civilian targets.

With a military resolution to the conflict seeming increasingly unlikely, and public support for the war declining in both Europe and the U.S., NATO members agreed in November 2010 to withdraw combat troops by 2014. The gradual transfer of security responsibilities to Afghan forces began in 2011. However, many observers questioned Afghan forces' ability to control the country after the withdrawal of NATO in 2014.

In 2014 Afghanistan held a presidential election to pick a successor to Karzai. As was widely expected, this was met with an upsurge of insurgent violence. Elections results were fraught with controversy over fraud. Finally, on September 21 Ashraf Ghani and Abdullah signed an agreement under which Ghani would become president and Abdullah or a nominee from his party would take the new position of chief executive officer.

CHAPTER TWO

WARS IN IRAQ

The Iraq War, also called the Second Persian Gulf War, was a conflict in Iraq that consisted of two phases. The first phase was a brief war in March–April 2003, in which a combined force of troops from the United States and Great Britain (with smaller groups from several other countries) invaded Iraq and rapidly defeated Iraqi military and paramilitary forces. A longer second phase involved a U.S.-led occupation of Iraq, which was opposed by an insurgency, or revolt. After violence began to decline in 2007, the United States gradually reduced its military presence in Iraq, formally completing its withdrawal in December 2011.

IRAQ'S OCCUPATION OF KUWAIT AND THE PERSIAN GULF WAR

Iraqi leader Saddam Hussein justified the 1990 invasion of Kuwait on grounds that Kuwait was historically part of Iraq. But the invasion was

Oil fields, such as Kuwait's Burgan oil field shown here, were destroyed as Saddam Hussein's troops retreated. Today many fields, including this one, have been rebuilt.

presumed to be motivated by Iraq's desire to acquire Kuwait's rich oil fields and expand its power in the region. The United States, fearing Iraq's broader strategic intentions and acting under United Nations (UN) auspices, eventually formed a coalition, which included a number of Arab countries, and began massing troops in northern Saudi Arabia. When Iraq ignored a UN Security Council deadline for it to withdraw from Kuwait, the coalition began a large-scale air offensive (Jan. 16–17, 1991). Saddam responded by launching ballistic missiles against neighboring coalition states as well as Israel. A ground offensive by the coalition (February 24–28) quickly achieved victory.

The Iraqi regime subsequently faced widespread popular uprisings, which it brutally suppressed. A UN trade embargo remained in effect after the end of the conflict, pending Iraq's compliance with the terms of the armistice. The foremost term was that Iraq destroy its nuclear, biological, and chemical weapons programs. The embargo continued into the 21st century and ceased only after the Iraq War started in 2003.

THE IRAQ WAR: SECOND PERSIAN GULF WAR

After Iraq's defeat, the Iraqi branch of the Baʿth Party, headed by Saddam Hussein, retained power by harshly suppressing uprisings of the country's minority Kurds and its majority Shīʿite Arabs. To stop Kurds from leaving Iraq, the allies established a "safe haven" in northern Iraq's predominantly Kurdish regions, and allied warplanes patrolled "no-fly" zones in northern and southern Iraq that were off-limits to Iraqi aircraft. Moreover, to restrain future Iraqi aggression, the United Nations (UN) implemented economic sanctions against Iraq to, among other things, hinder the progress of its most lethal arms programs, including those for the development of nuclear, biological, and chemical weapons. These weapons became known as weapons of mass destruction (WMD). UN inspections during the mid-1990s uncovered a variety of proscribed weapons and prohibited technology throughout Iraq. That country's continued flouting of the UN weapons ban and its repeated interference with the inspections frustrated the international community and led U.S. Pres. Bill Clinton in 1998 to order the bombing of several Iraqi military installations (code-named Operation Desert Fox). After the bombing, however, Iraq refused to allow inspectors to reenter the country. For several years the economic sanctions slowly began to erode as neighboring countries sought to reopen trade with Iraq.

THE WAR ON TERRORISM

In 2002 the new U.S. president, George W. Bush, argued that the vulnerability of the United States following the September 11 attacks of 2001, combined with Iraq's alleged continued possession and manufacture of weapons of mass destruction (an accusation that was later proved incorrect) and its support for terrorist groups—which, according to the Bush administration, included al-Qaeda, the perpetrators of the September 11 attacks—made disarming Iraq a renewed priority. UN Security Council Resolution 1441, passed on November 8, 2002, demanded that Iraq readmit inspectors and that it comply with all previous resolutions. Iraq appeared to comply with the resolution, but in early 2003 President Bush and British Prime Minister Tony Blair declared that Iraq was actually continuing to hinder UN inspections and that it still retained pro-scribed weapons. World leaders, such as French Pres. Jacques Chirac and German Chancellor Gerhard Schröder believed Iraq was cooperating and sought to extend inspections and give Iraq more time to comply with them. However, on March 17, Bush declared an end to diplomacy and issued an ultimatum to Saddam, giving the Iraqi president 48 hours to leave Iraq. The leaders of France, Germany, Russia, and other countries objected to this buildup toward war.

THE 2003 CONFLICT

When Saddam refused to leave Iraq, U.S. and allied forces launched an attack on the morn-ing of March 20; it began when U.S. aircraft dropped several precision-guided bombs on a bunker complex in which the Iraqi president was believed to be meeting with senior staff. Despite fears that Iraqi forces would engage in a scorched-earth policy—destroying bridges and dams and setting fire to Iraq's southern oil wells—little damage was done by retreating Iraqi forces; in fact, large numbers of Iraqi troops simply chose not to resist the advance of coalition forces. In southern Iraq the greatest resistance to U.S. forces as they advanced northward was from irregular groups of Ba'th Party supporters, known as Saddam's Fedayeen. British forces—which had deployed around the southern city of Al-Basrah—faced similar resistance from paramilitary and irregular fighters.

In March 2003 U.S.-led forces attacked the city of Baghdad, Iraq, from the air. The air strikes marked the beginning of the Iraq War.

In central Iraq units of the Republican Guard—a heavily armed paramilitary group connected with the ruling party—were deployed to defend the capital of Baghdad. As U.S. Army and Marine forces advanced northwestward up the Tigris-Euphrates river valley, they bypassed many populated areas where Fedayeen resistance was strongest and were slowed only on March 25 when inclement weather and an extended supply line briefly forced them to halt their advance within 60 miles (95 km) of Baghdad. During the pause, U.S. aircraft inflicted heavy damage on Republican Guard units around the capital. U.S. forces resumed their advance within a week, and on April 4 they took control of Baghdad's international airport. Iraqi resistance, though at times vigorous, was highly disorganized, and over the next several days army and Marine Corps units staged raids into the heart of the city. On April 9 resistance in Baghdad collapsed, and U.S. soldiers took control of the city.

On that same day Al-Basrah was finally secured by British forces, which had entered the city several days earlier. In the north, however, plans to open up another major front had been frustrated when the Turkish government refused to allow mechanized and armored U.S. Army units to pass through Turkey to set up in northern Iraq. Regardless, a regiment of American paratroopers did drop into the area, and U.S. Special Forces soldiers joined with Kurdish peshmerga fighters to seize the northern cities of Kirkuk on April 10 and Mosul on April 11. Saddam's hometown of Tikrit, the last major stronghold of the regime, fell with little resistance on April 13. Isolated groups of regime loyalists continued to fight, but the U.S. president declared an end to major combat on May 1. Iraqi leaders fled into hiding and were the object of an intense search by U.S. forces. Saddam Hussein was captured on December 13, 2003, and was turned over to Iraqi authorities in June 2004 to stand trial for various crimes; he was subsequently convicted of crimes against humanity and was executed on December 30, 2006.

IRAQI OCCUPATION AND CONTINUED WARFARE

Following the collapse of the Ba'thist regime, Iraq's major cities erupted in a wave of looting that was directed mostly at government offices and other public institutions. There were severe outbreaks of violence—both common criminal violence and acts of reprisal against the former ruling clique. Restoring law and order was difficult for the occupying forces, especially with continued attacks against occupying troops that soon developed into full-scale guerrilla warfare; increasingly, the conflict came to be identified as a civil war, although the Bush administration generally preferred the term "sectarian violence." Coalition casualties had been light in the initial 2003 combat, with about 150 deaths by May 1. However, deaths of U.S. troops soared thereafter, reaching some 1,000 by the time of the U.S. presidential election in November 2004 and surpassing 3,000 in early 2007; in addition,

several hundred soldiers from other coalition countries had been killed. The number of Iraqis who
died during the conflict is uncertain. One estimate
made in late 2006 put the total at more than
650,000 between the U.S.-led invasion and October 2006, but many other reported estimates put
the figures for the same period at about 40,000
to 50,000.

After 35 years of Baʿthist rule that included
three major wars and a dozen years of economic
sanctions, the economy was in shambles and only
slowly began to recover. Moreover, the country
remained saddled with debt that vastly exceeded
its annual gross domestic product, and oil produc-
tion—the country's single greatest source of reve-
nue—was badly hobbled. The continuing guerrilla
assaults on occupying forces and leaders of the
new Iraqi government in the years after the war
only compounded the difficulty of rebuilding Iraq.

In the Shīʿite regions of southern Iraq, many
of the local religious leaders (ayatollahs) who had
fled Saddam's regime returned to the country, and
Shīʿites from throughout the world were able to
resume the pilgrimage to the holy cities of Al-Najaf
and Karbala that had been banned under Saddam.
Throughout the country Iraqis began the painful
task of seeking loved ones who had fallen victim to
the former regime; mass graves yielded thousands
of victims. The sectarian violence that engulfed the
country caused enormous chaos, with brutal kill-
ings by rival Shīʿite and Sunni militias.

A CONTROVERSIAL WAR

Unlike the common consent reached in the Persian Gulf War, no broad coalition was assembled to remove Saddam and his Ba'th Party from power. Although some European leaders voiced their conditional support for the war and none regretted the end of the violent Ba'thist regime, public opinion in Europe and the Middle East was overwhelmingly against the war. Many in the Middle East saw it as a new brand of anti-Arab and anti-Islamic imperialism, and most Arab leaders decried the occupation of a fellow Arab country by foreign troops. Reaction to the war was mixed in the United States. Though several antiwar protests occurred in American cities in the lead-up to the invasion, many opinion polls showed considerable support for military action against Iraq before and during the war. Surprisingly, American opinions on the war sometimes crossed traditional party lines and doctrinal affiliation, with many to the right of the avowedly conservative Bush seeing the war as an act of reckless internationalism and some to the political left—appalled by the Ba'thist regime's brutal human rights violations and its consistent aggression—giving grudging support to military action.

As violence continued and casualties mounted, however, more Americans (including some who had initially supported the war) began to criticize the Bush administration for what they perceived to be the mishandling of the occupation of Iraq. The appearance in the news of photographs of U.S. soldiers abusing Iraqis at Abu Ghraib prison west of Baghdad—a facility notorious for brutality under the Ba'th regime—further damaged world opinion of the United States. In addition, a U.S. bipartisan commission formed to investigate the September 11 attacks reported in July 2004 that there was no evidence of a "collaborative operational relationship" between the Ba'thist government and al-Qaeda—a direct contradiction to one of the U.S. government's main justifications for the war.

Bush's prewar claims, the failure of U.S. intelligence services to correctly gauge Iraq's weapon-making capacity, and the failure to find any weapons of mass destruction—the Bush administration's primary rationale for going to war—became major political debating points. The war was a central issue in the 2004 U.S. presidential election, which Bush only narrowly won. Opposition to the war continued to increase over the next several years; soon only a dwindling minority of Americans believed that the initial decision to go to war in 2003 was the right one, and an even smaller number still supported the administration's handling of the situation in Iraq.

THE SURGE

Prior to the release of the Iraq Study Group report, there had been considerable debate within the administration over the path forward in Iraq. Although by December 2006 President Bush had indicated his inclination to increase the number of troops in Iraq, questions—in particular, the exact number of troops to be added—remained unsettled. Finally, in January 2007, President Bush announced a controversial plan to temporarily increase the number of U.S. troops there by more than 20,000, an effort that became known as the surge. Despite heavy casualties initially—2007 was

Iraqi soldiers, shown here, worked together with U.S. solders in air assaults, such as Operation Swarmer in March 2006. In December President George W. Bush was considering sending additional U.S. troops.

the deadliest year for U.S. forces since 2004—the drop in violence that occurred as the year drew on was a source of encouragement, and a number of the additional troops were subsequently withdrawn. The ultimate success of the surge itself remained a source of continuing debate, however, as the declining levels of violence observed in 2007 were attributed not solely to the surge itself but to a confluence of factors. Among these were a change in tactics that brought U.S. forces already on the ground more in line with classic counterinsurgency strategy; the Sunni Awakening, a movement in which Sunni tribesmen who had formerly fought against U.S. troops eventually realigned themselves to help counter other insurgents, particularly those affiliated with al-Qaeda; and the voluntary peace observed by the Mahdī Army (a Shī'ite military group) beginning in August of that year.

In November 2008 the Iraqi parliament approved a U.S.-Iraqi agreement that redefined the legal framework for U.S. military activity in Iraq and set a timetable for the final withdrawal of U.S. forces. Under the agreement, which was signed during the final months of the Bush administration after nearly a year of negotiation, U.S. troops were scheduled to leave the cities by mid-2009, and withdrawal from the country was set to be completed by Dec. 31, 2011. In February 2009 newly elected U.S. Pres. Barack Obama announced that U.S. combat forces would be withdrawn from Iraq by Aug. 31, 2010, with the remaining troops due to pull out by the end of 2011. On Aug. 18, 2010—two weeks ahead of schedule—the last combat brigade withdrew from Iraq; 50,000 U.S. soldiers remained in Iraq to act as a transitional force.

In contrast to publicly known U.S. military casualty figures (tracked by the Pentagon to more than 4,300 in October 2009), for a number of years no comprehensive data on Iraqi mortality was made available by the Iraqi government. In October 2009 the Iraqi government released its estimate of violent deaths for the 2004–08 period (statistics for the earliest portion of the war were far more difficult to obtain, due to the lack of a functioning government at that time). According to the government estimate, more than 85,000 Iraqis—a figure that included both civilians and military personnel—had died violently in the four-year period.

In July 2011, U.S. military officials announced that Iraq and the United States had begun nego-tiations to keep several thousand U.S. soldiers in Iraq past Dec. 31, 2011, the date for withdrawal set in negotiations in 2008. However, a possible extension of the U.S. presence in Iraq remained unpopular with the Iraq public and with several Iraqi political factions. Negotiations failed when the two sides were unable to reach an agreement over the continuation for U.S. troops of legal immunity from Iraqi law. In October, President

WIKILEAKS

In October 2010 the whistle-blowing organization WikiLeaks published nearly 400,000 secret U.S. military documents from the Iraq War online under the title "Iraq War Log," following the release of a similar cache of documents related to the Afghanistan War in July 2010. WikiLeaks made the documents available to several major news outlets, including *The New York Times, Der Spiegel, Le Monde, The Guardian,* and *Al-Jazeera* ahead of the publication date, stipulating that the material had to remain under embargo until the online release. The documents, mostly raw tactical and intelligence reports generated by field units in Iraq between 2004 and 2009, did not radically change the public understanding of the war, but they did reveal detailed information about its day-to-day conduct. They indicated that U.S. forces kept more detailed counts of Iraqi civilian casualties than previously acknowledged and that these counts indicated higher rates of civilian casualties than the military's public statements, that private military contractors were often involved in incidents of excessive force, that Iran provided extensive direct military aid to Shīʿite militias participating in Iraq's sectarian conflict, and that U.S.

forces ignored the widespread use of torture by Iraqi security forces. U.S. and Iraqi officials condemned the publication of the documents, saying that the release would set back security efforts and endanger the lives of military personnel and Iraqis who cooperated with the military.

Julian Assange founded the WikiLeaks website, which was responsible for publishing half a million U.S. military secret documents, many of which were related to the Iraq and Afghanistan wars.

Obama announced that the remaining 39,000 soldiers would leave the country at the end of 2011. The U.S. military formally declared the end of its mission in Iraq in a ceremony in Baghdad on December 15, as the final U.S. troops prepared to withdraw from the country.

CHAOS CONTINUED

As of 2014, Iraq continued to be in chaos despite the United States' help to create a new, democratically elected government there. An insurgent group, the Islamic State in Iraq and Syria (ISIS), made media headlines for its brutality. This group, comprised of Saddam Hussein loyalists and Islamic fundamentalists, overran large portions of the country. As ISIS cut through Iraq, major cities were threatened.

August 2014 was a critical month. When ISIS seized Mosul, Iraq's second-largest city, the United States resumed a role in Iraq for the first time since it withdrew troops in 2011. President Barack Obama authorized air strikes against militants in Iraq, hoping to prevent the fall of the Kurdish capital city, Erbil. He also authorized humanitarian assistance, including airdrops of food, water, and other supplies to help protect minority groups and other civilians who fled to safety into the mountains.

That same month, Iraqi prime minister Nūrī Kāmil al-Mālikī agreed to step down from his post with the goal of a peaceful transition to democratic elections without American military guidance. His successor, Haider al-Abadi, had the task of uniting the various and diverse groups, including the majority group of Shī'ites and the minority groups of Sunnis and Kurds, within Iraq

The 2014 beheading of journalist James Foley, shown here filming in Libya, was just one example of the shocking brutality exhibited by ISIS.

into a national government that could more effectively fight against the ISIS insurgents.

Also in August, ISIS beheaded James Foley,
an American journalist kidnapped two years earlier,
in retaliation for the American military strike. The
execution was videotaped, as was the beheading
of another American journalist, Steven Sotloff, in
September. These videos placed pressure on the
Obama administration to consider further military
action against ISIS in a strategy to contain the
insurgents.

Iraqi security forces continue to fight against
predatory ISIS militants as of March 2015.

CHAPTER THREE

KEY FIGURES IN THE WAR IN AFGHANISTAN

The Sept. 11, 2001, terrorist attacks on the United States were soon attributed to al-Qaeda, an Afghanistan-based extremist Islamic group led by notorious Osama bin Laden. So began a "war on terror" that played out on the world stage. The biographies of the following figures who were involved in the Afghanistan War highlight their backgrounds and the roles they played in the conflict. Along with bin Laden, biographies include his successor Ayman al-Zawahiri, Taliban leader Mohammad Omar, and U.S. figures General Tommy Franks, General Stanley McChrystal, and President Barack Obama.

ROBERT GATES
(1943–)

A specialist in security and intelligence, U.S. government official Robert M. Gates spent most of his career working his way up through the ranks of the Central Intelligence Agency (CIA). While earning a master's degree from Indiana University, he was recruited by the CIA. He served two years in the Air Force before join-ing the CIA full time as a Soviet analyst. In 1974 Gates received a doctorate in Russian and Soviet history from Georgetown University in Washington, D.C.

Gates then joined the staff of the National Security Council, serving under Presidents Richard Nixon, Gerald Ford, and Jimmy Carter until 1979, when he returned to the CIA. He rose to the post of deputy director of the agency in 1982. He served as deputy national security adviser to President George Bush from 1989 to 1991, when Bush nominated him for the CIA director's post again. Confirmed by the Senate in a 61–31 vote, Gates became the youngest director in the agency's history. His tenure ended little more than a year later, after Bill Clinton defeated Bush in the 1992 presidential election. In 1999 Gates was named dean of the George Bush School of Government and Public Service at Texas A&M University, and three years later he became president of the university.

Robert Gates served as secretary of defense in both the George W. Bush and Barack Obama administrations, as well as director of the Central Intelligence Agency, also under Bush.

In 2006 President George W. Bush appointed Gates secretary of defense. Gates had the reputation of a pragmatist who could assess a situation and respond accordingly. He was easily confirmed by the Senate in a 95–2 vote. In December 2008 Democratic President-elect Barack Obama selected Gates to continue as secretary of defense.

Gates retired in June 2011. Obama awarded Gates the Presidential Medal of Freedom later that year. Gates's memoir, *From the Shadows: The Ultimate Insider's Story of Five Presidents and How They Won the Cold War*, was published in 1996.

TOMMY FRANKS

(1945–)

Tommy Ray Franks is an American general who, as commander in chief of Central Command (Centcom; 2000–03), led U.S. forces in the overthrow of the Taliban regime in Afghanistan (2001) and of Saddam Hussein in Iraq (2003).

After graduating from the U.S. Army's Artillery Officer School in 1967, Franks rose through the ranks of the military until he was promoted in 2000 to commander of Centcom, the

organization responsible for all U.S. military operations in an area comprising 25 countries; at that time he also became a four-star general. The day after the September 11 attacks in the United States, Secretary of Defense Donald Rumsfeld ordered Franks to begin

Gen. Tommy Franks *(left)*, commander in chief of Central Command, with U.S. secretary of defense Donald Rumsfeld, 2002.

plans for retaliation. On Oct. 7, 2001, air strikes began against Afghanistan, which was harboring members of al-Qaeda, the Islamic militant group believed to be responsible for the attacks.

Though U.S. forces in Afghanistan failed to accomplish one of their major goals—capturing or killing al-Qaeda leader Osama bin Laden—the operation was deemed a success after the fall of the Taliban regime. Franks was then charged with overthrowing Saddam's regime in Iraq. On March 20, 2003, U.S. and allied forces launched an attack on Iraq and quickly toppled Saddam and his Ba'th Party. Despite this initial success, Franks's planning and execution of the invasion later drew criticism as the fighting continued. After 36 years in uniform, Franks retired in July 2003. Among many military honors he was awarded the Presidential Medal of Freedom, the highest U.S. civilian award, in 2004.

JAMES MATTIS
(1950–)

James Mattis joined the U.S. Marine Corps in 1972 and worked his way through the ranks, eventually being awarded multiple stars and other honors. After being promoted to lieutenant colonel, he deployed to the Persian Gulf as a part of Operation Desert Shield and commanded the 1st Battalion, 7th Marine Regiment, in the Persian Gulf War. As one of the lead assault elements of the 1st Marine

Division's Regimental Combat Team 7 (Task Force Ripper), Mattis's battalion was one of the first into Kuwait.

During the planning stages of the Afghanistan War, Mattis was chosen to lead Task Force 58, which was made up of two U.S. Navy amphibious readiness groups. He was the first marine to be given such a command. Afghanistan, a landlocked country, presented an obvious challenge to the amphibious assault forces, but Mattis brokered a secret agreement with the government of Pakistan to provide landing beaches and access to an airstrip. Task Force 58 was airlifted into Afghanistan in late November 2001 and was instrumental in the capture of Kandahār, a city regarded as the spiritual home of the Taliban.

Promoted to major general, Mattis led the 1st Marine Division during the early stages of the Iraq War, overseeing the longest sustained overland advance in Marine Corps history. The division returned to the United States in late 2003 but redeployed to Iraq the following year, Mattis led the marine assault on Al-Fallūjah.

He established the Center for Advanced Operational Culture Learning, a training academy for marine officers and senior enlisted personnel, to instill cultural awareness and language skills. After Gen. Stanley McChrystal was relieved as head of U.S. and NATO forces in Afghanistan in 2010, a command shuffle ensued. David Petraeus assumed McChrystal's role and Mattis replaced Petraeus as head of Centcom.

MOHAMMAD OMAR
(1950?–)

Biographical details about Mohammad Omar, also called Mullah Omar, are sparse and conflicting. Reportedly, he was born near Kandahār, Afghanistan, sometime between 1950 and 1962. He fought with the mujahideen against the Soviets during the Afghan War (1978–92). During that time he lost his right eye in an explosion.

After the Soviet withdrawal, political and ethnic violence continued to escalate. Claiming to have had a vision instructing him to restore peace, Mullah Omar led a group of madrasah students in the takeover of cities throughout the mid-1990s, including Kandahār, Herāt, Kabul, and Mazār-e Sharīf. In 1996 a shūrā (council) recognized Mullah Omar as amīr al-muʾminīn ("commander of the faithful"), a deeply significant title in the Muslim world that had not been used since 1924. This designation also made him emir of Afghanistan. The swift takeover of Afghanistan by the Taliban under Mullah Omar may have been funded at least partially by Osama bin Laden, who had moved his base to Afghanistan.

Under Mullah Omar's leadership, strict Islamic principles were enforced. Education and employment for women all but ceased; capital punishment for wrongdoings such as adultery and conversion away from Islam was enacted; and music, television, and other forms of popular entertainment were prohibited. He even ordered the destruction of the colossal

Buddha statues at Bamiyan, culturally significant relics of Afghanistan's pre-Islamic history, in 2001.

In the wake of the Sept. 11, 2001, attacks, Mullah Omar refused to extradite bin Laden. So the United States launched a series of military operations in Afghanistan. The Taliban government was overthrown, and Mullah Omar fled.

Mullah Omar was notoriously reclusive and meetings with non-Muslims or with Westerners were almost never granted. It is unclear whether any of the photographs supposedly depicting him are authentic. All this makes his capture even more difficult. At the end of the first decade of the 21st century, it was believed that Mullah Omar continued to direct Taliban operations from the sanctuary of Pakistan, although the Taliban denied it.

AYMAN AL-ZAWAHIRI
(1951–)

Ayman al-Zawahiri, who was born in Egypt in 1951, was a devout youth, and by age 15 he had established a group dedicated to the overthrow of the Egyptian government in favor of Islamic rule.

In the early 1990s Zawahiri took over as leader of the militant group Egyptian Islamic Jihad (thereafter better known as Islamic Jihad). Osama bin Laden had departed for Sudan in 1992, and Zawahiri ultimately joined him there. Sudan served as a base for training militants and for attacks on Egyptian targets, including attacks on government officials and on the Egyptian embassy in Pakistan. In June 1995 an unsuccessful attempt was made to assassinate Egyptian Pres. Hosni Mubarak himself. Under international pressure, the Sudanese eventually expelled Zawahiri and bin Laden, along with their followers.

Zawahiri's next movements are unclear. He appears to have traveled to European countries that included Switzerland, Bulgaria, and the Netherlands. In late 1996 he was arrested by Russian officials while illegally crossing the border en route to Chechnya, where he planned to launch a new base for Islamic Jihad. Although he was jailed for six months, Russian agents were apparently unaware of his identity until after his release.

In 1998 Zawahiri and bin Laden forged a formal alliance, and in June 2001 Islamic Jihad and al-Qaeda were merged. Zawahiri was closely affiliated with both the bombing of the USS *Cole* in October 2000 and the attacks of Sept. 11, 2001. Zawahiri gradually became al-Qaeda's chief spokesman, issuing commentary on issues such as the U.S. invasion of Iraq in 2003. In 2009 the U.S. Department of State determined that Zawahiri appeared to be al-Qaeda's leading decision maker, while bin Laden reportedly occupied figurehead status. Zawahiri assumed leadership of al-Qaeda in June 2011, following bin Laden's death during an American commando raid in Abbottabad, Pak., the previous month. In the years since, Zawahiri has released several videos, including one in September 2014 announcing that al-Qaeda would be establishing a presence on the Indian subcontinent.

STANLEY MCCHRYSTAL
(1954–)

Stanley McChrystal is a U.S. Army general who served as commander of U.S. and NATO forces in Afghanistan (2009–10). With the outbreak of the Persian Gulf War (1991), McChrystal was deployed to Saudi Arabia, and Joint Special Operations Command (JSOC) oversaw the search for Iraqi mobile Scud missile launchers. Shortly after the conflict he was promoted to lieutenant colonel.

McChrystal served as an officer in the U.S. Army from 1976. After the September 11 attacks of 2001, McChrystal—by that time a brigadier general—served as chief of staff to the combined joint task force operating in Afghanistan. In 2002 he was posted to the Pentagon as vice director of the Joint Staff, and in 2003 he assumed command of JSOC. During Donald Rumsfeld's term as secretary of defense (2001–06), increased importance was placed on the use of special forces units, and JSOC was tasked with high-profile missions during the Iraq War. McChrystal oversaw the capture of Saddam Hussein in 2003 and the air strike that killed al-Qaeda leader Abu Musab al-Zarqawi in 2006.

In June 2009, as the tide in Afghanistan appeared to turn against the United States, McChrystal was given command of the joint NATO-U.S. mission there. He received his fourth star within days of his appointment. Under McChrystal's command, the strategy in Afghanistan changed from the "light footprint"

Stanley McChrystal *(left)*, commander of U.S. and NATO forces in Afghanistan, and David Petraeus, commander in chief of Central Command, 2009.

counterterrorism operation to a complete counterinsurgency campaign. McChrystal requested the deployment of an additional 30,000 troops, which President Obama approved; this brought the total U.S. force commitment in early 2010 to almost 100,000 troops. McChrystal advocated a "hearts and minds" approach to interaction with the Afghan people, with the goal of reducing civilian deaths and promoting security and development at the local level. He was relieved of command in June 2010 after he and members of his staff made derisive comments about top Obama administration officials to a reporter from *Rolling Stone* magazine. In July McChrystal retired from the military. In 2011 he was appointed to a panel overseeing Joining Forces, a new government initiative to assist military families.

HAMID KARZAI
(1957–)

During the Afghan War, Hamid Karzai worked with

In January 2013, Afghanistan's President Hamid Karzai traveled to Washington, D.C., to meet with President Obama to discuss how the two countries could work together.

the mujahideen, who sought to overthrow the Soviet-backed government, and often traveled to the United States to seek support. When the communist government of Mohammad Najibullah fell in April 1992, the mujahideen established a coalition government, with Karzai serving as deputy foreign minister. In 1994, however, he resigned, tired of the infighting within the government. Conflict escalated until the mujahideen turned on one another, and in the ensuing turmoil, the Taliban came to power.

Although initially supportive of the Taliban and the order it introduced to the country, Karzai came to oppose the regime and again went into exile in Pakistan. In July 1999 his father was assassinated, an act that he blamed on the Taliban, and leadership of the Popalzai passed to Karzai. Shortly after the September 11 attacks in 2001, the United States led a military campaign to topple the Taliban and to capture terrorists that were based in the country. Karzai returned to Afghanistan to rally support for the U.S.-led mission, and by mid-November the Taliban regime had collapsed. To avert a destructive power struggle, representatives from various Afghan groups, aided by the international community, named Karzai chair of an interim admin-istration; he was sworn into office in late December 2001. In June 2002 a Loya Jirga, a traditional Afghan assembly, chose Karzai as president of a transitional government.

Violence continued to plague Afghanistan, and Karzai was the target of several assassination attempts. In January 2004 a new constitution was approved that called for a directly elected president. Later that year Karzai won the presidential election and was sworn into office.

Karzai enjoyed strong support from Western allies. But continued violence and instability and an inability to effectively build up Afghani institutions and provide basic services took its toll on his popularity, as did allegations of government corruption. In addition to increased drug trafficking—Afghanistan's opium-poppy harvest reached record levels in 2007—there was a resurgence of the Taliban, which mounted attacks with increasing frequency. Thus, pointed criticism began to emerge.

Karzai's term as president was due to expire in May 2009. After a contested election and a cancelled runoff election, Karzai was eventually inaugurated as president for a second term.

OSAMA BIN LADEN
(1957–2011)

The leader of a broad-based Islamic extremist movement, Osama bin Laden founded, directed, and financed a terrorist network known as al-Qaeda (which means "the Base" in Arabic). He was implicated in several deadly terrorist attacks against Western powers, including those of Sept. 11, 2001, against the United States, which killed more than 3,000 people.

Bin Laden was born in 1957 in Riyadh into one of the wealthiest families in Saudi Arabia. He joined the resistance fighters in Afghanistan after the Soviet Union invaded that country in 1979. Like many other Muslims worldwide, bin Laden believed it was his duty to help the Muslim Afghans drive out the occupying forces. He returned to Saudi Arabia after the Soviet troops withdrew in 1989.

Back home, bin Laden accused the Saudi government of corruption. During the Persian Gulf War, he denounced his government's decision to allow U.S. troops to establish bases in Saudi Arabia. Bin Laden formed al-Qaeda by 1993, mostly from men who had been his fellow resistance fighters in

Osama bin Laden founded the militant Islamist organization al-Qaeda and planned multiple attacks and suicide bombings against the United States, among other countries.

Afghanistan. After the Saudi government took away his passport in 1994, bin Laden fled to the Sudan. He established and ran terrorist training camps there until he was forced out of that country in 1996. Bin Laden later returned to Afghanistan, where he received protection from the Taliban-controlled government.

In a series of fatwas ("religious opinions") that he issued in 1996–98, bin Laden declared a holy war on the United States. He accused the country of supporting the enemies of Islam and despoiling Muslim countries of their natural resources, among many other charges. His ultimate goal was thought to be the creation of a single Islamic state, and he reputedly was trying to engage the United States in a large-scale war in which moderate Muslim governments would be overthrown.

Al-Qaeda recruited thousands of members worldwide. Among the terrorist acts attributed to the group are the bombing of the World Trade Center in New York City in 1993; the detonation of truck bombs against U.S. targets in Saudi Arabia in 1996; the killing of tourists in Egypt in 1997; the simultaneous bombing of U.S. embassies in Nairobi, Kenya, and Dar es Salaam, Tanzania; and the suicide bombing of the U.S. warship *Cole* in Aden, Yemen, in 2000.

Bin Laden was also believed to have masterminded the attacks of Sept. 11, 2001. In response, the United States led coalition forces in late 2001 that overthrew the Taliban in Afghanistan. U.S. forces hunted for bin Laden, but he escaped. Islamic extremist groups linked with al-Qaeda were blamed for deadly bombings in Bali, Indonesia, and Mombasa, Kenya, in 2002 and in Casablanca, Morocco, in 2003.

U.S. forces continued hunting bin Laden, who periodically released audio messages, many taunting the U.S. and the West. However, on May 1, 2011, President Obama reported that bin Laden had been killed in an action by U.S. forces in Abbottabad, Pakistan.

BARACK OBAMA
(1961–)

Barack Obama, in full Barack Hussein Obama II, was the 44th president of the United States and the first African American to hold the office. Before winning the presidency, Obama represented Illinois in the U.S. Senate (2005–08). He was the third African American to be elected to that body since the end of Reconstruction (1877). In 2009 he was awarded the Nobel Peace Prize "for his extraordinary efforts to strengthen international diplomacy and cooperation between peoples."

The wars in Afghanistan and Iraq were the main foreign-policy challenges for Obama's administration. He constantly spoke out in favor of focusing U.S. military efforts in Afghanistan rather than Iraq throughout his campaign for president.

As the Taliban experienced a resurgence in Afghanistan, the Obama administration conducted an intensive review of Afghan policy review. The president delivered a speech on December 1 in which

With the resurgence of the Taliban in Afghanistan, U.S. President Barack Obama announced a major escalation in the war there. He increased the number of troops there by 30,000 in 2010.

he announced a major escalation in the war effort. An additional 30,000 troops would be deployed to Afghanistan by the summer of 2010. The new strategy led to an increase in U.S. combat deaths; notably, during the first three months of 2010, U.S. deaths were approximately twice what they had been over the same period in 2009.

On April 4, 2011, Obama officially announced that he would seek reelection. Less than a month later, on May 1, the president made a dramatic late-night Sunday television address to inform the world that U.S. special forces had killed al-Qaeda leader Osama bin Laden in a firefight in a compound in Abbottabad, Pakistan, not far from the Pakistani capital of Islamabad. (U.S. forces took custody of the body, which they buried at sea, and confirmed bin Laden's identity through DNA testing.) "Justice has been done," Obama said. "Americans understand the costs of war. Yet as a country, we will never tolerate our security being threatened, nor stand idly by when our people have been killed. We will be relentless in defense of our citizens and our friends and allies."

CHAPTER FOUR

KEY FIGURES IN THE IRAQ WARS

Leading up to the September 11 attacks and in their aftermath, key American and Iraqi personalities emerged. American political leaders, especially those in the George W. Bush administration, had to make quick and tough decisions to protect democracy while launching the war against terrorism against the perpetrators of massive destruction. American generals were tasked to carry out strategic initiatives. The biographies that follow present insights into leaders who characterize the war on Iraq.

JAMES A. BAKER
(1930–)

American government official, political manager, and lawyer James Addison Baker held important posts in the Republican presidential administrations of the 1980s and early '90s. One of those positions was as U.S. secretary of state from 1989 to 1992 under President George Bush.

In 1970 Bush asked Baker, a longtime friend, to run his political campaign for the U.S.

Senate. Though Bush lost the race, Baker became deeply involved in Republican Party politics. Baker went on to direct Bush's campaign for the presidential nomination in the Republican primaries of 1980. After Bush accepted the vice presidential slot on a ticket headed by Ronald Reagan that year, Baker joined Reagan's campaign staff as a senior adviser. After Reagan won the election, he appointed Baker White House chief of staff, a post that Baker held until he was made secretary of the Treasury in 1985.

Baker managed Bush's successful campaign for the presidential election of 1988 and subsequently was appointed secretary of state. In that post Baker helped the United States reach agreement with the Soviet Union on the reunification of East with West Germany in 1990. In 1990–91 he helped orchestrate the international coalition that opposed Iraq's invasion of Kuwait. Baker was a shrewd and highly effective political manager whose skills helped the Republicans stay in control of the presidency throughout the 1980s. He resigned his post as secretary of state in 1992 to serve as White House chief of staff while simultaneously directing Bush's unsuccessful reelection campaign.

In the mid-2000s Baker participated on a number of government investigative committees; he served as cochair of both the Federal Commission on Election Reform (with former president Jimmy Carter) and the Iraq Study Group.

In 1991 Baker was awarded the Presidential Medal of Freedom. His memoir, *Work Hard, Study... and Keep Out of Politics!*, was published in 2006.

After working in government positions such as secretary of state, James Baker participated on investigative committees, such as the Iraq Study Group.

DONALD RUMSFELD

(1932–)

Donald Rumsfeld is a U.S. government official who served as secretary of defense (1975–77; 2001–06) in the Republican administrations of Presidents Gerald R. Ford and George W. Bush. Under President Ford, Rumsfeld served first as White House chief of staff (1974–75), then as secretary of defense (1975–77), the youngest person ever to hold that post. As defense secretary, Rumsfeld established the B-1 strategic bomber, the Trident ballistic missile submarine, and MX (Peacekeeper) intercontinental ballistic missile (ICBM) programs. After Ford's loss to Jimmy Carter, Rumsfeld entered the private sector.

In 2001 Rumsfeld became secretary of defense under President Bush. In addition to his continued support of a national missile defense system, he sought to modernize and streamline the military. Following the September 11 attacks later that year, Rumsfeld oversaw the U.S.-led attack on Afghanistan. It resulted in the overthrow of the Taliban, which was harboring Osama bin Laden—mastermind of the September 11 and other terrorist attacks against U.S. targets—and other al-Qaeda members. In March 2003 U.S. forces launched an invasion of Iraq. The regime of Iraqi Pres. Saddam Hussein was quickly toppled, and Rumsfeld initially earned praise for his handling of the war. However, as fighting continued, some accused him of deploying an inadequate number of troops. He faced further criticism in 2004 when photographs of U.S. soldiers abusing

Iraqi prisoners at Abu Ghraib prison in Baghdad were published. Following the 2006 midterm elections—in which the Republicans suffered heavy losses, in large part because of the growing opposition to the Iraq War—Rumsfeld announced his resignation. He was replaced by Robert M. Gates in December 2006.

JALAL TALABANI
(1933–)

Jalal Talabani is an Iraqi Kurdish politician who served as president of Iraq (2005–14). When the Kurds revolted against the government of ʿAbd al-Karīm Qāsim in 1961, Talabani joined the resistance. He led a successful campaign to force the Iraqi army out of the district of Sharbazher. Talabani subsequently undertook several diplomatic missions in Europe and the Middle East on behalf of the Kurdish leadership.

In 1975 Talabani and a group of Kurdish activists and intellectuals founded a new political party, the Patriotic Union of Kurdistan. During the late 1970s and early '80s, Talabani helped to organize Kurdish resistance to the Baʿthist regime of Iraqi leader Saddam Hussein. Saddam's successful military campaign against the Kurds (1987–88) forced Talabani to flee Iraq. Following the Persian Gulf War in 1991, Talabani returned to Iraq to help lead a Kurdish uprising against Saddam, which failed after U.S.-led forces refused to intervene to support the rebels. Talabani subsequently worked with the United States, the United Kingdom, Turkey, and France to establish

During the 2005 World Summit, Iraqi President Jalal Talabani addresses the UN General Assembly. Delegates occupy rows of seats with desks and can listen to translations of speeches through earphones.

a "safe haven" for Kurds in Iraqi Kurdistan in the far north and northeast of the country.

After the overthrow of Saddam in the 2003 Iraq War, Talabani became a member of the Iraqi Governing Council, which developed Iraq's interim constitution. In 2005 Talabani was elected interim president of Iraq by the National Assembly; he was reelected to a four-year term in 2006 and again in 2010. As president, Talabani worked to reduce sectarian violence and corruption within Iraq and to improve relations with Turkey, which had accused Iraq of allowing Kurdish rebels within Turkey to operate from bases in Iraqi Kurdistan. Talabani, suffering from poor health following a stroke in 2012, spent much of the last two years of his presidency receiving medical treatment in Germany. He was succeeded as president by another Kurdish politician, Fuad Masum.

COLIN POWELL
(1937–)

A four-star U.S. general and statesman, Colin Powell was the first African American to serve as chairman of the Joint Chiefs of Staff (1989–93) and secretary of state (2001–05). He oversaw the planning for the invasion of Panama (1989) and the Desert Shield and Desert Storm operations during the Persian Gulf War (1990–91). Powell retired from the military in 1993.

In 2000 President George W. Bush nominated Powell to become the 65th U.S. secretary of state. His nomination was unanimously confirmed by the U.S. Senate. Powell's tenure in the state department was beset with tensions, however, especially after the Sept. 11, 2001, terrorist attacks. His well-known preference for moderation and his view of war as "the politics of last resort" put him at odds with the Bush administration's overt moves toward an invasion of Iraq. The

Even after the Sept. 11, 2011, terrorist attacks, Colin Powell maintained that war was "the politics of last resort," which conflicted with the Bush administration's desire to invade Iraq.

Bush administration maintained that Iraq had links to al-Qaeda, the terrorist organization responsible for the September 11 attacks, and posed a direct threat to the United States. Although Powell was successful in persuading President Bush to present the case for intervention in Iraq before the United Nations (UN), much of the supporting evidence supplied in Powell's speech before the international body on Feb. 5, 2003, was later revealed to be false. In 2004 Powell testified before the Senate Governmental Affairs Committee that the sources of critical information relayed in his UN address were wrong. He also said that it was unlikely that any stockpiles of weapons of mass destruction, a keystone of the administration's case for the invasion of Iraq, would ever be found. Following the removal of Iraqi dictator Saddam Hussein, Powell worked to rally international support for the reconstruction of the war-torn country. He announced his resignation on Nov. 15, 2004.

SADDAM HUSSEIN
(1937–2006)

Saddam Hussein was born in 1937 to a peasant family in Tikrit, a village in northern Iraq. He joined the Ba'th party in 1957, and in 1959 he participated in an unsuccessful plot to assassinate 'Abd al-Karim Qasim, the Iraqi prime minister.

After the failed coup Saddam fled Iraq, going first to Syria and then to Egypt. He returned to

Baghdad in 1963 after Qasim was deposed and joined the Ba'th Party's new government. The new regime was short-lived, however—within months it was overthrown by 'Abd al-Salam 'Arif, a former Qasim ally. Saddam was arrested and imprisoned, but he escaped from confinement in 1966 and soon was elected to a prominent position in the Ba'th party.

During the 1970s Saddam continued to gain power. In 1979 he assumed the presidency after convincing the ailing President Ahmad Hassan al-Bakr to resign. Once in office, Saddam quickly ordered the execution of 22 high-ranking political rivals. He also established a secret police force to suppress political and popular opposition to his rule.

Relations between Iran and Iraq began deteriorating in the 1970s. Following a series of border skirmishes with Iran in 1980, Iraq launched a full-scale invasion of Iran's oil fields, bringing immediate retaliation by that country and initiating a war that lasted eight years.

During the Iran-Iraq War, Iraq used chemical weapons on Iranian troops as well as Iraqi Kurdish guerrilla fighters, who had joined the Iranian offensive. Although the use of these weapons had brought swift condemnation from the United Nations, in the late 1980s Saddam's regime ordered the use of chemical agents against Kurdish communities in northern Iraq. Thousands of civilians were killed, and many more sustained permanent health problems.

Saddam Hussein, shown here in 1987, was president of Iraq from 1979 to 2003. His rule was vicious, and he was eventually convicted of crimes against humanity.

By the late 1980s Iraq had accrued an enormous foreign debt from the cost of the Iran-Iraq War and its necessary interruption of oil exports. Despite this burden, Saddam continued to expand the military. In August 1990 Iraq invaded neighboring Kuwait, planning perhaps to use oil revenues from the energy-rich country to bolster its own economy. The move swiftly brought an international embargo against Iraqi oil. The United Nations (UN) condemned the occupation and authorized a military intervention to end it if necessary. In January 1991 a U.S.-led military coalition moved into the region; six weeks later, coalition forces had liberated Kuwait.

The UN cease-fire agreement that followed the Persian Gulf War prohibited Iraq from possessing biological, chemical, or nuclear weapons. Over the next decade, Saddam's refusal to cooperate with UN weapons inspectors brought worldwide economic sanctions and periodic air strikes by the United States and Great Britain. Finally, the United States and Great Britain in early 2003 warned Saddam of swift military action if disarmament was not completed promptly. In March 2003, U.S. President George W. Bush ordered Saddam to leave the country or face removal by force. Saddam refused to leave, and on March 20, 2003, a U.S.- and British-led coalition invaded Iraq. Saddam, along with his family and closest advisers, immediately went into hiding. Saddam eluded capture until Dec. 13, 2003, when U.S. troops discovered the former dictator in an underground hideout near his hometown of Tikrit. Although armed, Saddam surrendered without a struggle and was taken into custody.

In October 2005 Saddam went on trial before the Iraqi High Tribunal, a panel court established to try officials of the former Iraqi government. He and several codefendants were charged with the killing of 148 townspeople in Dujail, a mainly Shīʿite town in Iraq, in 1982. Throughout the nine-month trial, Saddam interrupted the proceedings with angry outbursts, claiming that the tribunal was a sham and that U.S. interests were behind it. In November 2006 Saddam was convicted of crimes against humanity, including willful killing, illegal imprisonment, deportation, and torture, and sentenced to death by hanging. Days after an Iraqi court upheld his sentence, Saddam was hanged in Baghdad on Dec. 30, 2006.

JOHN KERRY
(1943–)

In 2013 American politician John Kerry, who had served as a Democratic senator from Massachusetts for more than 25 years, resigned his position to become secretary of state under President Barack Obama.

After securing the Democratic Party's presidential nomination in 2004, Kerry chose John Edwards, a U.S. senator from North Carolina, as his running mate against incumbent President George W. Bush and Vice President Dick Cheney. Kerry called for greater diplomacy in foreign affairs and pointed to the Bush administration's failure to capture terrorist Osama bin Laden and to achieve peace in Iraq. The central campaign issue was Bush's response to the Sept. 11, 2001, terrorist attacks, an aggressive approach that split the country virtually down the middle.

Kerry had been launched into politics by his opposition to the Vietnam War in the early 1970s. As a U.S. senator, he had voted against the 1991 Gulf War, for the resolution authorizing the 2003 U.S.-led invasion of Iraq, but against an appropriation bill funding Iraq's occupation and rebuilding. At one point, attempting to explain, he noted that he had voted both for and against that funding bill—playing into Bush campaign charges that Kerry was an inveterate "flip-flopper." In an election with a huge voter turnout, Kerry and Edwards suffered a narrow defeat.

In December 2012 President Obama nominated Kerry to replace retiring Secretary of State Hillary Clinton, and Kerry was overwhelmingly confirmed by the U.S. Senate in January 2013. Since taking the office Kerry has been a controversial figure. Some say he is taking risks that will make great changes while others think his strategies will backfire. He has forcefully pushed for negotiation in the Mideast, breathed new life into the peace process between Israel and Palestine, and held high-level, in-person talks with top Iranian representatives. In November 2014, he met with Foreign Minister Yusuf bin Alawi of Oman in an effort to work out an Iranian nuclear agreement.

GEORGE W. BUSH

(1946–)

George W. Bush, the oldest son of former United States President George H. W. Bush, emerged from the shadow of his famous father to be elected president himself in 2000. A popular governor of Texas, Bush's combination of country-boy charisma and boundless enthusiasm eventually helped him win election as the country's 43rd chief executive. With his victory, he took his place alongside John Quincy Adams as the second son of a president also to serve in the office.

The terrorist attacks on Sept. 11, 2001, were a crisis that transformed Bush's presidency. Bush responded to the attacks by calling for a global war on terrorism. He worked to form an international coalition to combat terrorism using financial, legal, and political means as well as military force. In October 2001 Congress passed the administration's USA Patriot Act, which

U.S. President George W. Bush on Air Force One, Sept. 11, 2001.

gave the Federal Bureau of Investigation (FBI) and other law-enforcement agencies wide powers of search and surveillance in pursuing suspected terrorists, including great leeway in eavesdropping and detaining suspects. The act drew widespread criticism from civil liberties advocates. To coordinate efforts to protect the country against attacks, Bush created the Office of Homeland Security, which became a cabinet-level department in 2003.

The Bush administration blamed the September 11 attacks on al-Qaeda, an Islamic extremist group led by Osama bin Laden. On Oct. 7, 2001, U.S. and British forces began bombing Afghanistan, whose Taliban government was accused of harboring bin Laden and his followers. U.S. special forces were later deployed on the ground. By the end of the year al-Qaeda had been routed and the Taliban forced from power, though bin Laden had not been found. (He was eventually killed in a raid by U.S. forces in Pakistan in 2011.) Bush received high job-approval ratings among U.S. citizens for his response to the terrorist attacks and the war in Afghanistan.

In September 2002 Bush announced a new national security strategy that emphasized the need to defend against terrorists and "rogue states" that might threaten the country with "weapons of mass destruction"—biological, chemical, or nuclear arms. In a significant departure from past policy, the strategy declared that the country would take "preemptive" military action to prevent possible attacks. This position put the United States in conflict with much of the international community, especially most of Europe.

Critics of the preventive "first-strike" policy argued that it advocated acts of war that could violate international law. They also warned that it set a dangerous precedent for countries that might invoke a perceived threat as justification for military aggression.

Bush signaled his intention to put the new strategy into practice by identifying Iraqi President Saddam Hussein as a security threat. In late 2002 Bush accused the Iraqi government of possessing and developing weapons of mass destruction in violation of resolutions of the United Nations (UN) Security Council. In October 2002 the U.S. Congress passed a resolution authorizing Bush to use military force in Iraq. The administration then successfully lobbied the UN Security Council for a new resolution to send weapons inspectors to Iraq. In December, however, Bush declared that Saddam had failed to comply fully with the new resolution. The United States and its principal ally in the affair, the United Kingdom, tried unsuccessfully for several weeks to gain support from other Security Council members for a resolution that explicitly authorized military action against Iraq. Meanwhile, massive antiwar demonstrations were held in several major cities, especially in Europe.

Bush declared an end to diplomacy on March 17, 2003, giving Saddam 48 hours to step down and leave Iraq or face removal by force. After Saddam refused to leave, Bush ordered an invasion of Iraq, which began on March 20. By mid-April a coalition of mainly U.S. and British forces had entered all major Iraqi cities and overthrown Saddam's regime. Iraqi guerrilla attacks continued, however, and coalition forces lost control of many areas of the country. Meanwhile, investigations failed to produce evidence to support the administration's claims that Saddam had been developing weapons of mass destruction on a large scale.

ROBERT FISK
(1946–)

Robert Fisk is a British journalist and best-selling author known for his coverage of the Middle East. Fisk earned a B.A. in English literature at Lancaster University in 1968 and a Ph.D. in political science from Trinity College, Dublin, in 1985. He began his journalism career in 1972 as the Belfast correspondent of *The Times* of London, covering political turmoil in Northern Ireland. As the paper's Middle East correspondent from 1976 to 1987 he again reported on violent and tumultuous political events, such as the Lebanese civil war (1975–90), the Iranian Revolution (1978–79), and the Iran-Iraq War (1980–88). In 1989 Fisk moved to *The Independent*, where he continued to cover the Middle East from Beirut. He was known for his passionate reporting, his ability to secure access to frequently inaccessible people and places, and his willingness to brave danger to further his work. He was one of the few Western reporters to have interviewed al-Qaeda leader Osama bin Laden, a feat he accomplished three times during the 1990s. He also provided extensive coverage of the Persian Gulf War (1990–91), the U.S.-led war in Afghanistan (2001), and the Iraq War

(2003), priding himself on his eyewitness accounts while criticizing what he called the "hotel journalism" of some of his colleagues, which often relied heavily on official sources.

Fisk's reporting and commentary stirred controversy. His detractors questioned his journalistic impartiality, citing his opposition to the Iraq War and his criticism of U.S. and Israeli policies. His supporters, however, contended that most Western journalists are blindly supportive of the United States and Israel and that Fisk's work in comparison is almost uniquely objective and unbiased.

Fisk received numerous awards, including the British Press Awards International Journalist of the Year and Foreign Reporter of the Year. He wrote several books, including *The Great War for Civilisation— the Conquest of the Middle East* (2005).

NŪRĪ AL-MĀLIKĪ
(1950–)

Nūrī al-Mālikī joined the Daʿwah, an underground Shīʿite political party in 1963. In 1979, facing persecution from Saddam Hussein's regime, he left Iraq for Jordan and then moved to Syria and later Iran, where he arrived in 1982. The Iraqi government condemned him to death in absentia in 1980. Mālikī spent most of the decade of the Iran-Iraq War (1980–88) in Iran, and in 1989 he relocated to Damascus, where he became the head of the Daʿwah Party's Syrian branch.

In 2006 Nūrī al-Mālikī began his reign as prime minister of Iraq. His prime ministership was fraught with instability caused by violence and warfare between Sunni and Shīʿite militias.

After U.S.-led forces toppled the Ba'th regime in April 2003, Mālikī returned to Iraq. He became deputy head of the committee responsible for removing former Ba'th Party officials from government jobs and was elected to the Transitional National Assembly in 2005. In 2006 he became the new prime minister. He formed a government of national unity with a cabinet that included not only Shī'ite leaders but also members of the Arab Sunni, Kurdish, and secular blocs.

Unfortunately, Mālikī's prime ministership was unstable. The combination of warfare between Sunni and Shī'ite militias and a widespread anti-American and antigovernment insurgency created economic paralysis and a lack of security in the country.

In 2013 al-Qaeda in Iraq merged with some radical Syrian groups under the name Islamic State in Iraq and Syria (ISIS). In January 2014 the group began to take control of the majority-Sunni areas in western Iraq, forcing government troops to withdraw. In June ISIS fighters seized major cities in northern Iraq, prompting fears of a full-blown civil war.

The crisis was damaging to Mālikī, and in early August Haider al-Abadi, another member of the State of Law coalition, was nominated instead of Mālikī to form a new cabinet. Mālikī initially denounced Abadi's nomination as unconstitutional but relented when it became clear that he had lost much of his support.

ʿABD AL-ʿAZIZ AL-HAKIM
(1950–2009)

Iraqi political leader ʿAbd al-ʿAziz al-Hakim became head of Iraq's largest Shīʿite political party after years of opposing the regime of Saddam Hussein. Hakim was a member of a prominent clerical family that supported Shīʿite opposition political groups in Iraq and went into exile in Iran in 1980, shortly before the outbreak of the Iran-Iraq War (1980–90). In Iran, Hakim and his brother Ayatollah Muhammad Baqir al-Hakim established (1982) the Supreme Council for the Islamic Revolution in Iraq. While his brother chaired the organization, Hakim commanded its military arm, the Badr

Organization, which fought with Iran in the Iran-Iraq War. Both brothers returned to Iraq shortly after the U.S.-led invasion in 2003. In July of that year, Hakim became a member of the Iraqi Governing Council appointed by the Coalition Provisional Authority. When his brother was killed by a car bomb in August, Hakim took over the leadership of the Supreme Council for the Islamic Revolution in Iraq (from 2007, the Islamic Supreme Council of Iraq) and built the Shīʿite political coalition the United Iraqi Alliance, which came to power in the December 2005 elections for the Transitional National Assembly.

DAVID PETRAEUS
(1952–)

U.S. army general David Petraeus became a leader in the United States' war against terrorism. He headed multinational forces in Iraq from 2007 to 2008 and then served as commander in chief of Central Command (Centcom) from 2008 to 2010 and as commander of U.S. and North Atlantic Treaty Organization (NATO) forces in Afghanistan from 2010 to 2011. In 2011 he was nominated by President Barack Obama to become director of the Central Intelligence Agency (CIA), an appointment subsequently confirmed by the U.S. Senate.

Petraeus first led troops into battle as commander of the 101st Airborne Division during the U.S.-led invasion of Iraq in 2003. Following the end of major combat operations, the division was responsible for maintaining security and establishing democratic institutions in the northern city of Mosul. In 2004 Petraeus was chosen to head the Multi-National Security Transition Command and the NATO Training Mission, both in Iraq. In the latter role he was responsible for organizing and training Iraqi military and police forces. The next year Petraeus was appointed to head the U.S. Army Combined Arms Center at Fort Leavenworth, Kansas, home to several army training schools. While there, he coauthored the army's new official manual on counterinsurgency warfare.

In January 2007 President George W. Bush appointed Petraeus commander of the multinational forces in Iraq, and the Senate unanimously approved his nomination. He immediately began implementing a plan to secure Baghdad and the surrounding area. Petraeus, elevated to a four-star army general, sought to reduce levels of violence with an additional 30,000 U.S. troops to reinforce the 132,000 already fighting in Iraq. The increased troop levels—called for by the Bush administration—proved controversial as opposition to the Iraq War increased. Eight months after his appointment, Petraeus went to Capitol Hill to testify about overall progress in the war and reported that the incidence of violent attacks had declined substantially.

In April 2008 he was nominated to succeed Adm. William J. Fallon as head of Centcom, the organization responsible for all U.S. military operations in an area spanning 25 countries and stretching from the Horn of Africa through the Middle East to Central Asia. Petraeus was easily confirmed by the Senate in July. In September 2008 he stepped down as commander in

Iraq, and the following month he took charge of Cent-com. After Gen. Stanley McChrystal was relieved of his command in June 2010, Petraeus was named com-mander of U.S. and NATO forces in Afghanistan. The following year Pres. Barack Obama selected Petraeus to succeed Leon Panetta as director of the CIA; Petraeus was unanimously confirmed by the Senate in June. The following month he stepped down as commander in Afghanistan, and he retired from the military at the end of August. Petraeus was sworn in as director of the CIA a week later. In 2012 he resigned the post, citing an extramarital affair.

TONY BLAIR
(1953–)

On May 1, 1997, Tony Blair led the British Labour Party to a landslide victory in the House of Commons, hand-ing the Conservatives their worst loss since 1832. In foreign affairs, Blair allied the United Kingdom with the United States in a "war against terrorism" after the terrorist attacks against that nation on Sept. 11, 2001. Later that year, British troops joined U.S. and other allied forces in a war that overthrew the Taliban regime of Afghanistan.

Blair solidified the United Kingdom's position as the closest European ally of the United States with his vigorous support of a war against Iraq in spring 2003. Along with U.S. President George W. Bush, Blair accused Iraqi President Saddam Hussein of develop-ing chemical and biological weapons in violation of

United Nations Security Council resolutions. In the months preceding the war, Blair tried to convince both a divided public at home and the largely skeptical Security Council that weapons inspections were not working and that military action was justified. Meanwhile, worldwide antiwar demonstrations on Feb. 15, 2003, attracted record numbers of protestors, including more than a million in London. Many Labour Party members opposed the war, and several of Blair's cabinet ministers resigned. When the Security Council refused to pass a resolution explicitly authorizing force, Bush and Blair proceeded without its approval. U.S. and British forces began attacking Iraq in March 2003. They ousted Saddam's regime within a few weeks and began the difficult task of stabilizing and rebuilding the country.

In August 2003 Blair broke Clement Attlee's record as the longest continuously serving Labour prime minister in British history. Blair's popularity levels declined, however, amid allegations that he had misled the public about the threat posed by Iraq before the war. In early 2007 he announced that he would officially resign on June 27. He was subsequently selected to serve as special envoy to the Middle East.

CONDOLEEZZA RICE
(1954–)

U.S. educator and politician Condoleezza Rice was the first woman and the first African American

Condoleezza Rice became the first African American woman secretary of state. Previously she was the first woman and the first African American national security adviser in the United States.

national security adviser in the United States, serving from 2001 to 2005 under President George W. Bush. She became secretary of state in 2005, during that president's second term.

With a growing reputation as an expert on Soviet-bloc politics, in 1986 Rice became an adviser to the Joint Chiefs of Staff under President Ronald Reagan. During the administration of President George H.W. Bush, she was director and then senior director of Soviet and East European affairs on the National Security Council and a special assistant to the president. Rice returned to Stanford in 1991 and served as its provost from 1993 to 1999.

In 1999 Rice left Stanford to become foreign policy adviser to the presidential campaign of George W. Bush. Upon his becoming president, Bush made her national security adviser. After the terrorist attacks of Sept. 11, 2001, Rice supported the U.S.-led attacks on terrorist and Taliban targets in Afghanistan. She also advocated the overthrow of Iraqi president Saddam Hussein. When the administration drew criticism for the Iraq War, Rice vigorously defended the president's policies.

Early in 2005 Rice succeeded Colin Powell as secretary of state. In that post, she brokered negotiations to end Israel's occupation of the Gaza Strip and led the U.S. effort to promote peace between Israel and the Palestinians. She also persuaded North Korea to return to talks in which that country eventually agreed to dismantle its nuclear weapons program. In addition, Rice called for sanctions against Iran after that country did not end its nuclear program or allow inspections of its nuclear facilities. At the end of the Bush presidency in 2009, Rice returned to her academic career at Stanford.

SAMANTHA POWER
(1970–)

Samantha Power is an American journalist, human rights scholar, and government official who served on the National Security Council (2008–13) in the administration of U.S. President Barack Obama. In 2013 Power was nominated by Obama for the position of U.S. ambassador to the United Nations (U.S. Permanent Representative to the United Nations).

In her eyes, the lesson of the Holocaust and other genocides was that military intervention on humanitarian grounds was legitimate and necessary when a state committed atrocities against its own people and thereby lost its right to sovereignty. Power did not support all demands for humanitarian intervention but regarded the "immediate threat of a large-scale loss of life" as a standard for discriminating between such demands. She also stressed the importance for the United States of acting in concert with others through international institutions. Such standards, Power argued, had been met in the Persian Gulf War (1990–91) but not in the subsequent Iraq War (2003–11). In 2008 she published *Chasing the Flame: Sergio Vieira de Mello and the Fight to Save the World*, a biography of the Brazilian diplomat who, like her, sought to enlist governmental power in advancing human rights.

In 2005 Power met with Obama, then the junior senator from Illinois, to discuss her book *A Problem from Hell* and her views on American foreign policy. This meeting convinced her to leave Harvard to join Obama's staff as a foreign-policy adviser (2005–06). She was a senior foreign-policy adviser to Obama and actively campaigned for him during his 2008 bid for the presidential nomination of the Democratic Party.

After Obama's election in 2008 Power reentered his inner circle as Special Assistant to the President and Senior Director for Multilateral Affairs and Human Rights at the National Security Council, a body charged with advising the president on national security and foreign policy. In August 2013 Power replaced Susan Rice as ambassador to the United Nations.

MUQTADĀ AL-ṢADR
(1974–)

Muqtadā al-Ṣadr is an Iraqi Shīʿite leader and head of the militia known as Jaysh al-Mahdī (JAM), or the Mahdī Army. He was considered one of the most powerful political figures in Iraq in the early 21st century.

Ṣadr was the son of Grand Ayatollah Muḥammad Ṣādiq al-Ṣadr, one of the most prominent religious figures in the Islamic world. Ṣadr was greatly influenced by his father's conservative thoughts and ideas and by those of his father-in-law, Ayatollah Muḥammad Bāqir al-Ṣadr, founder of the Islamic Daʿwah Party, who in 1980 was executed for his opposition to Iraqi strongman Saddam Hussein.

Almost immediately after U.S.-led forces toppled Ṣaddam's regime in 2003, Ṣadr emerged from the shadows and began to open offices in his father's name (known collectively as the Office of the Martyr Ṣadr) in Baghdad, Al-Najaf, Karbalā', Al-Baṣrah, and other areas. He had immediate success in Madinat al-Thawrah (Revolution City), a poor Baghdad suburb of two million Shīʿites, which he renamed Ṣadr City in honor of his father. By the end of that year Ṣadr headed a Shīʿite political movement known as the Ṣadrist Movement and had attracted millions of Shīʿite followers across Iraq, mainly youth and the poor and downtrodden, to whom he offered a variety of social, educational, and health services. He also maintained tight security over the areas he controlled and established a court system based on Sharīʿah (Islamic law).

Ṣadr was accused of staging the murder of ʿAbd al-Majīd al-Khūʾī, a rival Shīʿite cleric, and a warrant for his arrest was issued but never executed. Ṣadr concentrated his rhetoric on Iraqi nationalism, especially the removal of U.S. forces from Iraq, and anti-Americanism. His militia, an ill-coordinated collection of thousands of outlaws, engaged in direct armed clashes with the multinational forces in April and August 2004 and was accused of contributing heavily to the ongoing civil conflict between Shīʿites and Sunnis. Ṣadr's critics held JAM responsible for brutal acts of retribution against Sunnis, including kidnapping, killing, torture, and the destruction of mosques and property.

Many Shīʿites regarded Ṣadr as a hero who opposed the Sunni rebels supporting al-Qaeda and who protected Shīʿites from Sunni insurgents. In the December 2005 election, members of Ṣadr's movement stood with other Shīʿite parties as part of the United Iraqi Alliance, which won a plurality of seats (128 of 275) in the parliament; 32 seats went to the Ṣadrists. In the formation of the government, Ṣadr supported Nūrī al-Mālikī of the Daʿwah Party for prime minister, but in April 2007 six Ṣadrist ministers withdrew from Mālikī's cabinet after their demands for a timetable for withdrawal of foreign troops remained unrealized. Also in 2007, possibly to escape increasing pressure from Iraqi security forces and the U.S. military, Ṣadr moved to Iran, where he entered a theological seminary in Qom while continuing to direct the actions of his followers in Iraq. In August Ṣadr made another tactical move, which coincided with the U.S. troop surge—he ordered that his militia suspend all activity for six months, during which time he intended to reorganize it in an attempt to restore its credibility. This suspension of all military activity was extended in late February 2008 for another six months, until August 2008. On March

25, however, the Iraqi government launched a military operation against Ṣadr's militia in Al-Baṣrah, and intense fighting ensued. The militia fought Iraqi troops to a standstill, and on March 30, following negotiations with government officials, Ṣadr ordered a cease-fire.

In August 2008 Ṣadr's plan to reorganize his militia was realized in the launch of al-Mumah-hidūn ("Those Who Pave the Way"), an unarmed wing of JAM that Ṣadr declared would focus on social and religious programs; only a small, specialized portion of the original Mahdī Army was to remain armed. A complete restructuring into a solely social organization, including dissolution of the organization's remaining armed branch, was made contingent upon the implementation of a timetable for U.S. withdrawal from Iraq. Shortly thereafter Ṣadr announced the indefinite extension of the cease-fire that had been put in place the previous year.

In 2010, following months of political stalemate after a close parliamentary election left the main factions in Iraq unable to form a government, Ṣadr paved the way for a resolution by agreeing in negotiations to endorse Mālikī for the position of prime minister. The Ṣadrists secured a number of concessions from Mālikī in return for their support, including several posts in the new cabinet. In January 2010, possibly capitalizing on his increased political stature, Ṣadr unexpectedly returned from exile in Iran to his home city of Al-Najaf.

CONCLUSION

In September 2014 Haider al-Abadi took the seat as prime minister of Iraq with an endorsement from U.S. President Barack Obama as a good replacement for Nūrī al-Mālikī. Al-Abadi immediately made moves to rebuild the country. Amid car bombings and reports of beheadings, in November 2014 the U.S.-led air campaign against ISIS seemed to be finally having some effect. Air strikes in Iraq and Syria have resulted in the deaths of hundreds of ISIS fighters. In and around Kobani, Kurdish fighters reportedly made additional progress in their defense of the Syrian town. Iraqi troops have also made gains, such as taking back areas close to Baiji and surrounding Iraq's largest oil refinery. Still, U.S. President Barack Obama ordered another 1,500 troops to go to the country earlier that same month.

Afghanistan is not necessarily beyond the reach of ISIS, either. According to reports in November 2014, ISIS had overtaken a city in Libya, causing concern among leaders that areas in Afghanistan, as well as Pakistan and India and beyond, could be threatened by ISIS fighters in the not-too-distant future.

Although both Iraq and Afghanistan have withstood unimaginable adversity, both continue to move forward. Among the ruins of war in

Afghanistan in Kabul, for example, a new amusement park opened in November 2014. Kabul City Park's Ferris wheel, roller coaster, and other rides offer what seems like a colorful symbol of hope and a respite from the harsh and wearisome war.

GLOSSARY

clique A narrow exclusive circle or group of persons; especially one held together by a presumed identity of interests, views, or purposes.

coalition The union of things separate into a single body or group.

counterinsurgency Organized military activity designed to combat insurgency.

counterterrorism The measures taken to combat terrorism.

deploy To extend (a military or naval unit) in width or in both width and depth.

diplomacy The art and practice of conducting negotiations between nations to achieve terms that are satisfactory to all.

emir A nobleman, independent chieftain, or native ruler especially in Arabia and Africa, often used as a title.

faction A party, combination, or clique (as within a state, government, or other association) often contentious, self-seeking, or reckless of the common good.

fatwas Legal opinions or decrees handed down by an Islamic religious leader.

guerrilla warfare Irregular military actions (such as harassment and sabotage) carried out by small usually independent forces.

insurgent A person who rises in revolt against civil authority or an established government.

Labour Party A major political party of the United Kingdom in the 20th century associated with socialistic policies (as the nationalization of basic industries) and characterized by an organization in which trade unions are predominant.

madrasah A Muslim school, college, or university that is often part of a mosque.

Marxist-Leninist Follower of a theory and practice of communism developed by or held to be developed by Lenin from the doctrines of Marx.

mujahideen Islamic guerrilla fighters especially in the Middle East.

paramilitary Existing where there are no military services or existing alongside the military services as a possible support or diversion.

peshmerga Armed Kurdish forces.

rogue Of or being a nation whose leaders defy international law or norms of international behavior.

sanctions Formal decrees.

shah The sovereign of Iran.

sham A trick that deludes.

tribunal A court or forum of justice.

Afghanistan World Foundation

35 East 21st Street, 10th Floor

New York, NY 10010

(212) 228-3288

Website: http://www.afghanistanworldfoundation.org

The Afghanistan World Foundation is dedicated to assisting reconstruction and development in Afghanistan. It promotes awareness of Afghans' struggles through events, media resources, and international partnerships.

Embassy of Afghanistan

2341 Wyoming Avenue NW

Washington, DC 20008

(202) 483-6410

Website: http://www.embassyofafghanistan.org

The official U.S.-based representation for Afghanistan offers information and assistance to Americans seeking to do business in or travel to Afghanistan.

Embassy of Afghanistan in Canada

240 Argyle Avenue

Ottawa, ON K2P 1B9

Canada

(613) 563-4223

Website: http://www.afghanemb-canada.net

The Embassy of Afghanistan in Canada is Afghanistan's official representation in Canada.

Embassy of the Republic of Iraq

3421 Massachusetts Avenue NW

Washington, DC 20007

(202) 742-1600

Website: http://www.iraqiembassy.us

The Embassy of the Republic of Iraq "serves as a link between the Republic of Iraq and the government and people of the United States of America."

United States Institute of Peace: Afghanistan

Website: http://www.usip.org/category/countries/afghanistan

The United States Institute of Peace has been promoting peace and stability in Afghanistan since 2002. It established an office in Kabul in 2008, which provides events and programs in the country.

United States Institute of Peace: Iraq

2301 Constitution Avenue NW

Washington, DC 20037

(202) 457-1700

Website: http://www.usip.org/category/countries/iraq

Since 2003, the United States Institute of Peace: Iraq
has been working to support Iraqi efforts to prevent and resolve disputes peacefully.

WEBSITES

Because of the changing nature of Internet links, Rosen
Publishing has developed an online list of websites
related to the subject of this book. This site is updated
regularly. Please use this link to access the list:

http://www.rosenlinks.com/WAR/Iraq

Burgan, Michael. *Barack Obama* (Front-Page Lives). Chicago, IL: Heinemann Library, 2010.

Burgan, Michael. *George W. Bush* (Presidents and Their Times). New York, NY: Marshall Cavendish Benchmark, 2012.

Etheredge, Laura S. *Iraq* (Middle East in Transition). New York, NY: Britannica Educational Publishing, 2011.

Gerber, Larry. *The Taliban in Afghanistan.* New York, NY: Rosen Publishing, 2010.

Gerszak, Rafal, and Dawn Hunter. *Beyond Bullets: A Photo Journal of Afghanistan.* Toronto, ON: Annick Press, 2011.

Hollar, Sherman. *Barack Obama* (Pivotal Presidents: Profiles in Leadership). New York, NY: Britannica Educational Publishing, 2013.

Langley, Andrew. *Bush, Blair, and Iraq: Days of Decision.* Chicago, IL: Capstone Heinemann, 2014.

Lusted, Marcia Amidon, and David C. Rappaport. *The Capture and Killing of Osama bin Laden* (Essential Events). Edina, MN: ABDO Publishing, 2012.

Miller, Mara. *The Iraq War: A Controversial War in Perspective.* Berkeley Heights, NJ: Enslow Publishing, 2011.

Price, Sean. *Osama bin Laden.* Oxford, UK: Heinemann Library, 2010.

Rice, Condoleezza. *Condoleezza Rice: A Memoir of My Extraordinary, Ordinary Family and Me.* New York, NY: Ember, 2012.

Zullo, Allan. *War Heroes: Voices from Iraq.* New York, NY: Scholastic, 2009.

A

Abadi, Haider al-, 37, 84, 96

Abdullah, Abdullah, 18, 19

Abu Ghraib prison, 30, 65

Afghanistan, Soviet invasion of, 11–12, 55

Afghanistan War
accelerated American involvement, 18–19

phases of, 10

presidential elections, 17–18

U.S.-British invasion, 12–15

Alawi, Yusuf bin, 75

'Arif, 'Abd al-Salam, 71

B

Badr Organization, 84–85

Baker, James, 61–62

Bakr, Ahmad Hassan al-, 71

Ba'th Party, 22, 25, 27, 28, 29, 30, 44, 65, 70, 71, 83

Blair, Tony, 23, 87–88

Bush, George H.W., 40, 61, 62, 76, 90

Bush, George W., 8, 23, 24, 29–30, 31, 32, 42, 61, 64, 68, 70, 73, 74, 75, 76–80, 86, 87, 88, 90, 91

C

Carter, Jimmy, 40, 62, 64

Center for Advanced Operational Culture Learning, 45

Chasing the Flame: Sergio Vieira de Mello and the Fight to Save the World, 91–92

Chirac, Jacques, 24

Clinton, Bill, 23, 40

Clinton, Hillary, 75

Cole, USS, 48, 57

D

Da'wah Party, 81, 93, 94

E

Edwards, John, 74, 75

Egyptian Islamic Jihad, 47

F

Fallon, William J., 86

Fisk, Robert, 80–81

Foley, James, 38

Ford, Gerald, 40, 64

Franks, Tommy, 39, 42–44

From the Shadows: The Ultimate Insider's Story of Five Presidents and How They Won the Cold War, 42

G

Gates, Robert, 39–42, 65

Ghani, Ashraf, 19

Great Britain/United Kingdom, 8, 11, 15, 20, 25, 65, 73, 78, 79, 87–88

Great War for Civilisation—the Conquest of the Middle East, The, 81

H

Hakim, 'Abd al-'Aziz al-, 84–85

Hakim, Ayatollah Muhammad Baqir al-, 84

Homeland Security, Office of, 78

I

Iran-Iraq War, 71–73, 84, 85

Iraq

continued chaos in, 36–38

Iraq War: Second Persian Gulf War, 20, 22–23

occupation and continued warfare, 27–28

occupation of Kuwait and the Persian Gulf War, 20–22, 62, 73

opposition to war and controversy, 29–30

the surge, 30–36

2003 conflict, 24–27

and war on terrorism, 23–24

ISIS, 9, 36–38, 84, 96

Islamic Jihad, 47, 48

Islamic Supreme Council of Iraq, 85

K

Karzai, Hamid, 15, 17–18, 19, 51–55

Kerry, John, 74–75

Kurds, 22, 26, 37, 65–67, 71, 83, 96

Kuwait, invasion of, 20–22, 62, 73

L

Laden, Osama bin, 8, 12–15, 39, 44, 46, 47, 48, 55–58, 60, 64, 75, 78, 80

M

Mahdi Army/JAM (Jaysh al-Mahdī), 32, 92, 94, 95

Mālikī, Nūrī Kamil al-, 36–37, 81–84, 94, 95, 96

Massoud, Ahmad Shah, 12

Masum, Fuad, 67

Mattis, James, 44–45

McChrystal, Stanley, 39, 45, 49–51, 87

Mubarak, Hosni, 48

mujahideen, 12, 46, 53

N

Najibullah, Mohammad, 53

Northern Alliance, 12, 13, 15

O

Obama, Barack, 10, 17, 18, 32, 33–36, 37, 38, 39, 42, 51, 58–60, 74, 75, 85, 87, 91, 92, 96

Omar, Mohammad, 39, 46–47

Operation Desert Fox, 23

Operation Desert Shield, 44, 68

Operation Desert Storm, 68

P

Pakistan, 11, 13, 45, 47, 48, 53, 58, 60, 96

Petraeus, David, 45, 85–87

Powell, Colin, 68–70, 90

Power, Samantha, 91–92

Problem from Hell, A, 92

Q

Qaeda, al-, 8, 10, 12, 17, 23, 30, 32, 39, 44, 48, 49, 55–58, 60, 64, 70, 78, 80, 84, 94

Qāsim, ʿAbd al-Karīm, 65, 70, 71

R

Reagan, Ronald, 62, 90

Republican Guard, 26

Rice, Condoleezza, 88–91

Rice, Susan, 92

Rumsfeld, Donald, 43, 49, 64–65

S

Saddam Hussein, 20, 22, 24–27, 28, 29, 36, 42, 44, 49, 64, 65, 67, 70–74, 79–80, 81, 84, 87, 88, 90, 93

Ṣadr, Ayatollah Muhammad Baqir al-, 93

Ṣadr, Grand Ayatollah Muḥammad Ṣādiq al-, 92

Ṣadr, Muqtada al-, 92–95

Ṣadrist Movement, 93

Saudi Arabia, 11, 13, 21, 49, 55, 57

Schröder, Gerhard, 24

Sept. 11, 2001, attacks, 6–8, 10, 12, 13, 23, 39, 43, 47, 48, 49, 54, 55, 57, 61, 64, 68, 70, 75, 76, 78, 87, 90

Shīʿites, 22, 28, 32, 34, 37, 74, 81, 83, 84, 85, 93, 94

Sotloff, Steven, 38

Sunni Awakening, 32

Sunnis, 28, 32, 37, 83, 84, 94

Supreme Council for the Islamic Revolution, 84, 85

T

Taliban, 8, 10, 12, 13, 15, 17, 19, 39, 42, 44, 45, 46, 47, 53, 54, 57, 58, 64, 78, 87, 90

Talibani, Jalal, 65–67

U

United Iraqi Alliance, 85, 94

USA Patriot Act, 76–78

W

weapons of mass destruction (WMD), 22–23, 30, 70, 73, 78, 79, 87

WikiLeaks, 34–35

Work Hard, Study...and Keep Out of Politics!, 62

Z

Zarqawi, Abu Musab al-, 49

Zawahiri, Ayman al-, 39, 47–48